School of the Prophets Advanced Course

Diving Into the Mysteries of the Prophetic

BY DR. JEREMY LOPEZ

THE TRAINING MANUAL FOR THE SCHOOL OF THE PROPHETS

Identity Network International, Inc.

www.identitynetwork.net

P.O. Box 383213 Birmingham, AL 35238

205-362-7133

Copyright © 2013 by Dr. Jeremy Lopez
School of the Prophets Advanced Course

A Training Manual

All rights reserved. No part of this book may be reproduced in any form or by any electronic or mechanical means including information storage and retrieval systems - except in the case of brief quotations embodied in critical articles or reviews - without permission in writing from the author.

Printed and bound in the United States of America.

ISBN 978-1-300-78501-9

Acknowledgement:

Dedicated to all who desire to hear the voice of the Lord. I pray everyone has clarity on hearing the voice of the Good Shepherd.

A special thanks to **Jim and Jeanne Lopez**. Their love towards me as parents has been an anchor in my life. Thanks so much for your support and love.

I would also like to thank the staff of Identity Network for making this project possible.

Table of Contents:

Part 1: Are You Ready for Your Impartation?

Part 2: The Power of the Voice Within

Part 3: Prophetic Imagination is Creation

Part 4: The Law of Preparation

Part 5: The Combination Factor: Understanding the Process of Transformation

Part 6: Metamorphosis Transformation

Part 7: Christ Consciousness

Part 8: The Process of Prophetic Leading

ARE YOU READY FOR YOUR IMPARTATION?

Are You Ready for your Impartation and Activation?

When we deal with the power of impartation and activation, we are dealing with the power of movement. Impartation and activation are action words. This means, the power of impartation comes upon us through some type of movement that happens willingly or not willingly; simply because, our minds pick up on everything that surrounds us in the moment. And when we "pay attention" to something and incorporate our focus into that substance or conversation, it becomes a part of us then. This is why it is so important to keep a watch over what we see, feel and hear. When we move in the mind of Christ, we allow the power of impartation to be a part of our daily lives through the things the Lord brings us every day. His voice holds life-giving seed!

Now many people have heard it said that the power of impartation comes from someone who lays hands upon us and imparts something to us. Paul tells us in the book of Romans a little more about the power of impartation.

Romans 1:1 *"I long to see you so that I may impart to you some spiritual gift to make you strong...."*

This statement is true but it does not hold the only avenue. Even as someone gives a prophetic word to you by laying hands upon you, you can also catch with your ears, mind and spirit something someone says over you or to someone else and your mind can grab a hold of their words and impregnate you through the power of impartation.

Once again, impartation comes in many different forms and ways. Anything your spirit grabs a hold of, it begins to grow in the very fibers of our being. We begin to receive the seed of that conversation, idea or substance. We have to remember, that our spirit and mind can draw to itself anything it feels or desires it needs on the journey of life. Now in dealing with the power of impartation, even though we can grab a hold and receive what someone says over us or about us, it does not mean it will come to pass unless we allow the law of activation to give it life. In the Old Testament, we read about King David who is going through a very hard time and the Bible says that David encouraged himself in the Lord.

1 Samuel 30:6 *"And David was greatly distressed; for the people spake of stoning him, because the soul of all the people was grieved, every man for his sons and for his daughters: but David encouraged himself in the Lord his God."*

In 1 Samuel chapter 30, we see David began, through the power of activation, resurrect the power of encouragement within his life. Once I begin, through the power of desire and attention, give life to anything that comes to me, I begin to activate it to work inside of me. The word "encourage" in the Hebrew means to, *"rebuild, repair and put back together."*

1. Repair
2. Rebuild
3. Put back together

So you see, you can have hands laid upon you for someone to move by the law of impartation and prophesy the word of the Lord to you, but it does not mean it will take place or happen with in your life. In fact, just because someone lays hands upon you, does not mean you've even had an impartation without attention, focus and desire.

1. Attention
2. Focus
3. Desire

These three elements feed into the power of activation within a person's life.

We have to realize in our lives, that all of creation and everything God sets into motion in the universe is governed by what we think within our heart.

Proverbs 23:7 *"For as he thinketh in his heart, so is he: Eat and drink, saith he to thee; but his heart is not with thee."*

The thoughts and intents of the heart cause things to become life within us. When we begin to move in our prophetic gift, we must understand how the law of activation and the law of impartation work. Everything God brings into our lives, once they have our focus, it begins a Genesis effect within us. The prophetic word of the Lord once spoken into our lives or from our mouths to someone else, even though it is a seed of life given by the Father, will not happen unless we give it our heart, soul and strength; which is basically our entire focus and desire in life. The power of impartation is always accelerated within us to give and receive when we move in the mind of Christ, by giving it *His* full desire and passion as well.

Jacob and Laban

Jacob and Laban had an agreement that Jacob could have all the spotted flocks for what Laban basically owed him. Jacob made a very wise move in getting the flocks to have spots. When the flock was in heat and getting ready to mate, Jacob put pieces of bark within the trough where they drank from the water when eating. When the flock saw the "spots" in the water, they bore forth what they beheld!

31 *"What shall I give you?" he (Laban) asked. "Don't give me anything," Jacob replied. "But if you will do this one*

thing for me, I will go on tending your flocks and watching over them: 32 Let me go through all your flocks today and remove from them every speckled or spotted sheep, every dark-colored lamb and every spotted or speckled goat. They will be my wages. 33 And my honesty will testify for me in the future, whenever you check on the wages you have paid me. Any goat in my possession that is not speckled or spotted, or any lamb that is not dark-colored, will be considered stolen." 34 "Agreed," said Laban. "Let it be as you have said."

Now read in verse 38 and 39:

38 "Then he placed the peeled branches in all the watering troughs, so that they would be directly in front of the flocks when they came to drink. When the flocks were in heat and came to drink, 39 they mated in front of the branches. And they bore young that were streaked or speckled or spotted."

Prophetic Principle:

Whatever you Behold, you will Become.

In other words, in the power of activation and impartation, you must see yourself or behold the "you" the prophetic word or impartation said you now have become. Impartation only happens when you "believe that you have received it and you shall have it."

Mark 11:24 *"Therefore I tell you, whatever you ask for in prayer, believe that you have received it, and it will be yours."*

The power is in the "beholding" stage that welcomes you to "come and dine" in it; so you will become it. If you want to activate your impartation; believe the impartation over you from that moment on and you shall be it.

Questions
Part 1

1. Impartation and activation are _____ words.

2. The only way to receive an impartation is by the laying on of hands. (T or F)

3. By paying attention and giving your full _____ to something, it causes you to receive an impartation.

4. His voice holds life-giving _____!

5. John the Baptist tells us some things in the book of Romans about the power of impartation (T or F)

6. Impartation comes in different ways; so be careful what you ___, _____ and _____.

7. The word "encourage" in the Hebrew language means to, _____, _____ and ___ ____ _____ _____.

8. What are the three elements to cause the power of impartation to come alive in your life?
   _____
   _____
   _____

9. When we give our focus to something, a _____ effect takes place within us.

10. Moving in the mind of Christ always causes an _____ in the impartation because it brings in His passion to the situation.

11. Explain your personal experience of how you ever received an impartation?

The feeling during the impartation:
_____

The knowledge gained for it:
_____

Explain how the anointing felt during an impartation as opposed to an anointing from worship:
_____
_____

THE POWER OF
THE VOICE WITHIN

The Power of the Voice Within

So many people in my life ask me, how do you hear the voice of God? I always share with them, ① there isn't an actual formula to hear his voice but you must be open by having an ear to hear and an eye to see.

Revelation 2:7 *"Whoever has ears, let them hear what the Spirit says....."*

This basically means that you must be open-minded beyond yourself. We are so full of ourselves, that many times even in a one on one conversation with someone else, even though it appears we are hearing them, we are not.

Genesis 27:8 *"Now, my son, listen carefully and do what I tell you."* ②

Many times, we are too busy hearing ourselves of how we are to respond to the person that is presently speaking to us that we shut them out by automatically thinking about what we are going to say once they finish their statement. I always share with people, you must begin to be a good listener to others before you can begin to understand His ways and His thoughts when He speaks to you.

John 10:27 *"My sheep hear my voice, and I know them, and they follow me."* ④

I totally believe you must have a prayer life and a time of devotion and meditation before the Lord. But you must also walk in an awareness.

Awareness - *"the state or condition of being aware; having knowledge; consciousness."*

Awareness speaks of not just being conscious of what is within, but you must also be conscious of what is outside of yourself and your mind. The voice of the Lord can come to us in many forms. Many people beat their head against the wall because they're trying to hear the voice of the Lord in the same way Jeremy Lopez does or how someone else hears His voice. But we have to remember that the Lord speaks even to prophets in many different ways at many different times. In other words, many times I hear the word of the Lord in my spirit before my mind even hears the word of the Lord for someone else. Sometimes there is a bubbling forth in my spirit of what the Lord desires to say to someone else and yet I have no clue what is about to come out of my mouth. So many times it can bypass even my natural mind. There are many times I also get what I like to call a "gut feeling." Many Christian people throw out the phrase, "gut feeling" simply because it is not a Christianese term. But we must remember, it is the Lord delivering the message to us, not us bringing the message to ourselves.

The Power of the Word

✱ Inside of the prophetic word as it is placed on the inside of you are the nutrients that your life lacks in order to fulfill your destiny.

Nutrients - *"Nourishing; providing nourishment or nutriment."*

When we begin to step into the word of the Lord, we must become the word of the Lord; which means, the prophetic word will hover over you waiting for you to accept it and then become it. The prophetic word has the hidden resources you need to not just live a good life, but to put you over the edge into the Zoe kind of life. Zoe means, "the God kind of life."

John 10:10 *"The thief cometh not, but for to steal, and to kill, and to destroy: I am come that they might have life, and that they might have it more abundantly."*

✱ The prophetic word will thrust you into the "abundance of life" you were meant to live in. The "nutrients" your life has been lacking has now been made available for you to partake of. The power of the word of the Lord brings all the things from the kingdom of God that religion has taken from our treasure within. Inside of us is a treasure in our earthen vessel. This treasure is full of the Zoe of God.

> ### Prophetic Principle:
>
> (17) When we begin to Expand our Consciousness, which is our Mind, by Extending the Borders of our Imagination, We will Give an Entrance to the Lord to Speak to Us by Any and Every means Possible.

2 Corinthians 4:7 *"But we have this treasure in earthen vessels, that the Excellency of the power may be of God, and not of us."*

And every time religion and traditions of men that make the word of God of none effect impregnates us with its poison, our treasure begins to fall asleep inside of us and we forget who we are in Christ more and more every day.

Mark 7:13 *"Making the word of God of none effect through your tradition, which ye have delivered: and many such like things do ye."*

God's prophetic word awakens us and speaks life into us by saying, "Let there be Light." Light drives out the darkness and shows us the "Christ in us, the hope of glory."

Genesis 1:3 *"And God said, 'Let there be light,' and there was light."*

God's voice thunders in every vein of our body and causes the blood to pump with clarity. His voice in us breaks to pieces the hardest of hearts, cleanses the lepers and restores our soul. Just one word can change our lives forever.

Psalms 29:3-9 *"The voice of the Lord is upon the waters: the God of glory thundereth: the Lord is upon many waters. 4 The voice of the Lord is powerful; the voice of the Lord is full of majesty. 5 The voice of the Lord breaketh the cedars; yea, the Lord breaketh the cedars of Lebanon. 6 He maketh them also to skip like a calf; Lebanon and Sirion like a young unicorn. 7 The voice of the Lord divideth the flames of fire. 8 The voice of the Lord shaketh the wilderness; the Lord shaketh the wilderness of Kadesh. 9 The voice of the Lord maketh the hinds to calve, and discovereth the forests: and in his temple doth every one speak of his glory."*

His word takes our minds to places of creativity that supersedes any earthly invention ever created. Once we step into and become what the word says and is, we begin to see the inner court (spirit) and outer court (body) of our lives radically altered as if it were a planet getting back on its correct axis.

Questions:
Part 2

1. There is not an actual _____ to hearing the voice of the Lord.

2. Genesis 27:8 "*Now, my son, _____ carefully and do what I tell you.*"

3. How do you hear the voice of the Lord for yourself?
   _____

4. As a believer in Christ, do all believers hear His voice?
   _____

5. (Answer this definition) "The state or condition of being _____; having knowledge; consciousness."

6. People will hear the voice of the Lord the same way since His voice is the same. (T of F)

7. When we begin to expand our _____, we will see the entrance of the heavens open up to us.

8. The prophetic word will _____ over you until you accept it and _____ it.

9. "Zoe" means, "The normal kind of life." (T or F)

10. Explain what it is that takes away the word of the Lord and causes it to be void in the earth.

_____

PROPHETIC IMAGINATION IS CREATION

Prophetic Imagination is Creation

When we studied the book of Genesis in chapter 1, we begin to understand the power of creation through a spoken word. We began to understand that God spoke a word into nothingness.

Genesis 1:1-3 *"In the beginning God created the heavens and the earth. 2 Now the earth was formless and empty, darkness was over the surface of the deep, and the Spirit of God was hovering over the waters. 3 And God said, "Let there be light," and there was light. 4 God saw that the light was good, and he separated the light from the darkness."*

Which means God's voice and His word speaks something into nothing. When we begin to move and breathe in the prophetic imagination, we begin to understand there is creation within our mouths. Creation comes through a word. When we begin to stir up our imagination, we will begin to be more creative. This does not mean we will add to the prophetic word of the Lord that God has given us. But it will help bring forth the beauty, the correct emotion, and the picture that God desires to set up within us.

> *Prophetic Principle:*
>
> The Creative Mind is a Powerful Tool.

God has created our minds to have thoughts and picture forms. Pictures do tell 1,000 words. And when we begin to move in the stages of the Genesis effect in our imagination, we will begin to understand the power that can be birthed when we open our mouths and speak.

- Life exists within your prophetic word.
- The seed of purpose is within the prophetic word.

I know of so many people, that when they work on their job, they begin to tap into a source and supply that is not from the human mind. The mind of God is something we should daily walk in and not out of. Imagery of ourselves that takes place within our mind, determines how we will walk, behave, and talk. Remember, everything starts within a seed, which is a thought within the mind. Once a thought from the imagination begins to be magnified by us feeding into it, it begins to manifest in our natural world. This is why it is so important to understand and realize that thoughts become things, and what I think I will become.

But because I live in a fallen world, my mind began to be tainted by religion. Other people began to affect who I am, what I am, and where I will be in the future. When we keep our minds focused on the Author and Finisher of our faith, which is the Lord, and move within His mind, nothing in life is impossible for me to achieve and accomplish.

Prophetic Principle:

When the Imagination of Man begins to Tap into the Presence of the Spontaneous Prophetic Flow of God Almighty, Nothing will be Impossible for Us to Accomplish and Achieve.

My world is created by my thoughts and my imagination.

God said basically, you have what you say. In essence, this means what I say, comes from a thought planted in my mind first and foremost. Being prophetic means I move in the spontaneous power of the now since God's name is I AM and not "I will become" or "I used to be." The power of the prophetic is a spontaneous flow that does not come from a limited, natural world; but comes and flows from the heavenly realms.

Questions:
Part 3

1. Everything in creation was created by a _____ ____.

2. Creation comes through a ____.

3. When we begin to move in the stages of the _____ _____ in our imagination, we will begin to understand the power that can be birthed when we open our mouths and speak.

4. When the imagination of man begins to tap into the presence of the spontaneous prophetic flow of God Almighty, nothing will be impossible for us to accomplish and achieve. (T or F)

5. When I was born, my mind was _____ for _____.

6. My world is created by my _____ and my imagination.

7. Explain how your mind works and how you need to change it to hear God more:
_____
_____

8. Being prophetic means I move in the spontaneous ____ __ ___ ___; since God's name is I AM and not "I will become" or "I used to be."

9. The power of the prophetic is a spontaneous flow that does not come from a limited, natural world; but comes and flows from the _____ _____.

10. Because I live in a fallen world, my mind can be tainted by religion. Explain in your own words how religion can be destroyed within your own life:
_____
_____

THE LAW OF PREPARATION

The Law of Preparation

The Bible speaks a lot about preparation. In fact, Matthew, Mark, Luke and John all discuss the power of the sixth day. According to the Gospels, the sixth hour and the sixth day tend to have a common denominator to them. It was considered to be the day of preparation.

Examples in scripture of the 6th day in dealing with preparation:

John 19:14 *"And it was the preparation of the Passover, and about the sixth hour: and he saith unto the Jews, Behold your King!"*

Mark 15:42 *"And now when the even was come, because it was the preparation, that is, the day before the sabbath...."*

Luke 23:54 *"And that day was the preparation, and the sabbath drew on."*

Any time you have a birth or a death, the law of preparation needs to be present. So any time within your life you are in getting a new job or possibly you desire a new car, you must always use wisdom and allow yourself to prepare before the manifestation. Many times in our lives, when we receive the word of the Lord through a prophetic utterance, we must always prepare and get ready for its delivery or birthing. The reason why it takes around nine months for a woman to bear forth a child is because she must be in preparation for its delivery. If a woman conceives the seed of a man and has the birthing of her child the very next morning, it would not only take her by surprise but she would have nothing for her infant. Every time the word of the Lord comes to us, He always leaves room for preparation.

Joseph of Arimathea

Even after the Lords death, the man by the name of Joseph, which is from Arimathea, took the body of Christ and carried it through a time frame of preparation by wrapping his body up in fresh linen.

Matthew 27:57-61 *"57 As evening approached, there came a rich man from Arimathea, named Joseph, who had himself become a disciple of Jesus. 58 Going to Pilate, he asked for Jesus' body, and Pilate ordered that it be given to him. 59 Joseph took the body, wrapped it in a clean linen cloth, 60 and placed it in his own new tomb that he had cut out of the rock. He rolled a big stone in front of the entrance to the tomb and went away. 61 Mary Magdalene and the other Mary were sitting there opposite the tomb."*

So you see, from birth to death, there is always a preparation time. When we receive the word of the Lord, through a prophetic utterance or dream, we must allow the law of preparation to take its course in our lives. In the time frame of your preparation, wisdom will begin to knock on your door to carry you through the process so your delivery will be a success. When people ask me how I can prepare to see my prophecy come to pass, I always let them know that during your time of preparation you will need to expand the borders of your imagination and realize your life has just shifted and will never be the same again.

Prosperity must begin in the mind first in order to prosper and see the fulfillment of your word manifest outwardly.

3 John 1:2 *"Beloved, I wish above all things that thou mayest prosper and be in health, even as thy soul prospereth."*

Prophetic Principle:

Know the Season you're Currently Operating in.
Never Go into the "Now" Moment Blinded.

If your mind does not prosper or go to a higher plane of imagination in order to not only fit in this new birthing within your life, but to allow creativity to become the new "baby's" best friend. I always share with people, to make sure that the word of the Lord that is coming into your life happens, you must always introduce this new birthing (baby-prophecy)to creativity. Anything that comes into my life that has been birthed from the Lord, I always allow or stir up my creative levels to give full attention to the new birthing. Remember, everything in your life will grow. Whether it is good or bad or by the power of your attention, your prophetic word will grow in the direction you focus on. This is why it is so important to make sure you keep your focus on things of the Lord so your prophetic word will grow "towards" the perfect will of God for your life instead if growing away from His will.

Philippians 4:8 *"Finally, brothers, whatever is true, whatever is noble, whatever is right, whatever is pure, whatever is lovely, whatever is admirable--if anything is excellent or praiseworthy--think about such things."*

So you may ask the question, how do I introduce creativity to my new birthing? The power of creativity is stirred up when you begin to take your new birthing and imagine it in its fullest grown form. Make sure you always give it attention by "feeding" into it with the imagination. Remember when your first child was born? Remember how you gave it attention, fed it, clothed it, etc.? How you would sit there and daydream of your boy becoming a football player or your little girl would grow up to be a cheerleader? This is the same way you treat your prophetic word. Once the prophetic utterance is released in the atmosphere, it looks for someone who will receive it, give it life by helping form it with their thoughts and feed it by the power of creative imagination. Things manifest in the natural only when it is "old enough" and mature to stand on its own. If it is not fed creativity when received into your spiritual womb, if born, it will have the nutrients it lacks to complete the task at hand. Through this malnourished process, it will take a lot longer to process and complete its mission in your life since it is now "mentally challenged." When you feed your prophetic utterance, once received, it can make great accomplishments for the kingdom of God. Everyone knows that every creature waiting to be a "new born" must have proper nourishment, care and tender loving in order for it to be healthy and live a good, long productive life.

Below is a list of some questions that I always ask and imagine my prophetic word will be as it grows and matures in my life.

1. I imagine the outcome of my word.
2. I imagine what it will look like.
3. I feed my attention into it.
4. I begin to work the rest of my life around the prophetic word, not my prophetic word around my life.

You see, preparation involves a lot of different things and God will present you with the things you will need in order to make your birthing come to pass. Sometimes, preparation can bring with it many emotions.

Many times, a woman gets very excited and can express joy, excitement, laughter and even nervousness. But your preparation time is a season you will never forget. Preparation time allows you the change you need to make in order to see your prophetic word come to pass. When anything new comes into our lives, we must always allow the law of preparation to consume us. It causes each and every one of us to take a deep breath and savor the moment. The law of preparation, when allowed in our lives, always introduces us to a great wisdom we never knew before.

Questions:
Part 4

1. The sixth hour or the 6th day tends to represent in the New Testament, the day of _____.

2. Any time you have a _____ or a _____, the law of _____ needs to take place.

3. When you are in the process of getting a new item such as a car or house, etc., you must make the preparation in order for the _____ to take place.

4. Know the season you're currently operating in. Never go into the "_____" moment blinded.

5. Your mind must _____ in order to go to a higher plane.

6. When you are about to receive the word of the Lord or have just received a prophetic word, you always need to introduce your baby (prophetic word) to _____. Because _____ and your baby (prophetic word) should become good friends.

7. Things _____ in the natural only when it is "old enough" and mature to stand on its own.

8. When your prophetic word is "malnourished" from the bomb, it will take a lot longer to process and complete its mission in your life since it is now "mentally challenged." (T or F)

9. Name four things you would imagine to help empower the fulfillment of the word of the Lord within your life:

1. _____
2. _____
3. _____
4. _____

10. Your _____ time is a season you will never forget.

THE COMBINATION FACTOR -
UNDERSTANDING THE PROCESS OF TRANSFORMATION

The Combination Factor - Understanding the Process of Transformation

$$\frac{7}{9} + \frac{3}{18}$$

$$\frac{4}{12} + \frac{1}{4}$$

$$\frac{2}{21} + \frac{2}{7}$$

In dealing with the combination factor of the prophetic, I want to read 2 Kings 15:12 *"This was the word of the Lord which he spake unto Jahu saying, thy sign shall see it on the throne of Israel unto the fourth generation, and so it came to pass."*

One of the main things we try to understand within the combination of the prophetic is exactly how does it work.

The prophetic utterance has a certain combination factor just like a combination on a lock. In order to get into the lock you must first know the numeric code to know how to turn it to the left or turn it to the right in order to cause the combination to open and release itself that you may dive into the lock and receive the goods that were presently held from you. The main words I want us to focus on today are the words, "and it came to pass."

With every Alpha, there must be an Omega

Matthew 7:28 *"And it came to pass, when Jesus had ended these sayings, the people were astonished at his doctrine..."*

This phrase, "and it came to pass," lets us know and understand that the fulfillment of what He said, is completed today. You have reached your Omega stage of this word. In other words, there is always an Omega when there is an Alpha. In your life there is always a beginning to something and there will always be an ending as well. The problem with most people is we never understand that in the middle of what I like to call "meta," which means among or between, there is a combination factor. Many people go through their lives trying to figure out what lies ahead of them. And yet others go through their lives not really caring, just going with the flow of life. But going with the flow of life means you will receive whatever is dropped in your lap. This means, you have no control over your own destiny, life or anything else that happens to you. But the Bible makes it very plain that Jesus holds the keys. So if we are bone of His bone and flesh of His flesh, we are one with the Father and hold the same keys in our hands too.

It is the same for a married couple, they both can write a check from the same checkbook. He will put Mr. Jones and she has the legal right to put Mrs. Jones since the nation considers them the same. Since Jesus is the husbandman; that would make us the bride of Christ. So as the bride of Christ, we have access to His authority, power, and anointing.

> *Prophetic Principle:*
>
> You Must know and Understand the Combination to Your Destiny. Just like A Lock, Every Numeric Code is Different. Yours is fashioned just for You.

The Bible says, that the same spirit that raised Christ from the dead, dwells within me; which means there is a life-giving spirit that dwells within me. This Holy Spirit has the force or drive to resurrect anything in my life that is dead.

Ask, Seek, Knock

So as we see in our previous paragraph, we come to the understanding that we can no longer just allow life to lead us but we are called to seek and find the answer we're looking for. We are called to ask and it shall be given. We are called to knock upon the door and the solution we are looking for will be found.

Matthew 7:7 *"Ask, and it shall be given you; seek, and ye shall find; knock, and it shall be opened unto you."*

I like to call the "journey" the combination factor. In the prophetic discipline, when we receive a prophetic word, many of us do not know how that prophetic word will come to pass. But we have to understand that there is a combination factor to anything and everything that life brings us. That is why we are commanded to ask and it shall be given, seek and we shall find, knock and the door shall be opened. And it is the exact same within the prophetic realm.

> ### Prophetic Principle:
>
> The Words, *"And it Came to Pass"* Holds A Lot of Power.

The Combination Lock

When you receive a prophetic word, or even give a prophetic word, in the middle of that prophetic word, there will be a combination lock. And that combination lock holds a certain numeric code that is not hidden from you, but it is hidden for you to find and discover. There are many questions that we must ask ourselves today. And I would like to give you a minimum of three questions you need to ask yourself.

- We need to know, when dealing with a prophetic word, "How it should happen?"
- The second question you need to ask yourself is, "When should it happen?"
- And the third question we need to ask ourselves is, "How do I discover the combination to unlock the destiny of the prophetic word within me?"

Faith and the Prophetic

Many times in life, when we receive a prophetic word, we always want to set our own combination factor to our prophetic word. Which means, we want to be in control and use our own natural knowledge, which I like to call our "safety zone" because it's what we know with our natural mind. Because of the fact that if I can set my own combination factor to the prophetic word I just received, then I won't have to work so hard to get the answer. I will have to strive very hard and step outside of my comfort zone in order to make it happen. But you see, the prophetic dimensions of the kingdom of God, holds a great mystery called faith.

Hebrews 11:1 *"Now faith is the substance of things hoped for, the evidence of things not seen."*

This means faith goes hand in hand with the prophetic dimension.

Romans 12:6 *"Having then gifts differing according to the grace that is given to us, whether prophecy, let us prophesy according to the proportion of our faith."*

You see, we do not hold the combination factor to our prophetic word. Simply because, God desires for us as humans to step out of ourselves and cast our nets into the deep waters. You see as Christians the nets we were given are not called to cast into the shallow waters, but they are called and can only be used for the deepest part of the waters.

Mathematic Discipline

Within, what I like to call the mathematic discipline, there are codes, sequences and certain patterns that causes numbers to find whatever combination or answer it is looking for. This means if you are looking for a particular number, there will be many combination factors to reach that specific number.

Let me give you an example:

If we are trying to reach the number five for example, we must realize there is more than one way to reach the number five through many different avenues dealing with numbers.

Examples to reach the number 5:

$4 + 1 = 5$
$3 + 2 = 5$
$5 \times 1 = 5$
$10 \div 2 = 5$

So you see, there are many different avenues or combinations to reach a certain destiny. And as we seek and ask the Holy Spirit to find out which combination factor that has our name written on it in order to fulfill our destiny, we must go beyond the normal into the supernatural to discover what we are looking for. As we see above, there are at least four different avenues or combination factors to reach the number five. So it is within the prophetic language of the prophetic dimension of your word. So as we examine the four different dimensions or avenues to reach the number five, as shown above, we must discover which certain avenue God desires for us to feel our destiny within the prophetic word to reach the number or goal that is hailed within the perfect will of God for our lives.

You see, we have to allow God to hold the combination factor. When God holds the combination factor it means He strategically plans the combination code within the prophetic word so when it reaches the receivers spirit, it challenges the mind and the soul of a man to begin a journey to find its way back home.

There is an old saying that says, "different strokes for different folks." Every lock that is hailed within a prophetic word has a different "combination code" buried deep in the heart of it.

It means something has broken through. As if it were a chicken finally hatching from the egg in which it has been buried for so long. When a seed is planted in the ground, as we look at the seed, we do not see its potential. And the seed itself has no clue what it will become. But it knows deep down inside of it, it holds the greatest potential to be something bigger than it's ever imagined or thought possible. When we take a look at the acorn, we do not have a clue that it has the potential and yet it holds the reality that it will one day be one of the largest trees, which we call an oak tree. You see the prophetic word works the exact same way. Within the prophetic word, lays a destiny that goes beyond anything a person can think, ask, or imagine. A prophetic word houses something that is greater than you and I. It holds substance that the world has never seen before. The Scripture says, *"To call those things that be not as though it were."* So the prophetic word holds something that has never produced, or has ever been seen with the human eye in this natural world. But yet, it is smart enough to know, by the mind of Christ in which it takes its directions from, that it cannot be easily accessed by any human reasoning, nor can it be broken into by the wisdom of man. But the only way to understand the very mind of God buried deep within the seed or the word of the Lord, it must take something from a world in which many of us have fallen asleep towards, which is the spirit realm.

The problem with most people, who have received prophetic words in their lives is that they have no clue how to get to the stage, or should I say the last stage of the prophetic word to make it a common reality and manifest it within their lives.

The main reason why many people never reach the last stage where their prophetic word comes to pass, is simply because they suffer from a lack of knowledge of what to do next.

And that knowledge does not come through the means of a man or a woman, but it can only be tapped into or accessed by and through the mind of Christ.

Questions:
Part 5

1. One of the main things we try to understand within the _____ of the prophetic is exactly how does it work.

2. On a lock, there is a certain _____ _____ you must know in order to unlock the lock.

3. There is always an Omega when there is an Alpha. (T or F)

4. The Words, "___ __ ____ __ ____" Hold A Lot of Power.

5. There is a _____ _____ to anything and everything that life brings us.

6. What goes hand in hand with the prophetic dimension? _____

7. We _____ according to the proportion of our faith.

8. Tell me your experience of how your prophetic word came to pass? In other words, what was the key for you that "made it happen?"
   _____
   _____

9. In the _____ _____, there are codes, sequences and certain patterns that causes numbers to find whatever combination or answer it is looking for.

10. There are many different _____ or _____ to reach a certain destiny.

11. You cannot see the _____ of the seed when it is buried in the ground.

12. A _____ _____ houses something that is greater than you and I.

METAMORPHOSIS
TRANSITION

Metamorphosis Transition

Metamorphosis is the actual process we will go through within this life whenever we receive a greater revelation than our current self. Any time you receive something greater than the way you think, you will always be stretched, plowed, and transformed. Just like the caterpillar turns into a butterfly, so is it when the word of the Lord starts working within our lives to transform us into His image and likeness.

The caterpillar begins to go through so many changes from restructuring to having certain cells begin to die and other cells beginning to awaken.

When we talk about a transformation factor, we literally mean a rebirthing or a transfiguration that will take place within your life, to get you where the greater revelation is held. It literally means to change in form or nature. It begins to redefine you, or bring to you a new definition or should I say the original definition in which you were created to be in this life. You see before you were ever in your mother's womb, you had an encounter with the most high God. It means there was an importation given to you before you were ever born. This importation was spoken of in the book of Jeremiah chapter 1.

The Transformation Process has Begun

So once we receive the word of the Lord, which comes from the mind of Christ, which is higher than the mind of man, we will go through a metamorphosis transformation. **Change will Occur**; which means, it will change your character, purpose, circumstance, and every situation you are presently in. We have to understand and realize, that the person who received the prophetic word, which is you, will not be the same person who will fulfill the word. That means through a transformation or metamorphosis process, you will be changed into a new person. Because the prophetic word received will take you through a metamorphosis process to get you back to your original state of being, which is the real you that God formulated and created while you were on the potter's wheel before the world ever began. There is a real you that has been covered up by the validation of man, what others have said about you, and through the fears that you have created for yourself to be accepted by other people. The prophetic word has come to set you free and get you back to your original state of being.

Everything Built Up must Now be Broken Down

Everything within my life that I have built up, through my own hand or by the hand of others, must now come down. Everything in creation has a cycle, of life and death. We see that through the four seasons every year. We see the winter season, the spring season, the summer season, and the fall season. And these four seasons make up the cycle within the earth. Everything that is born must die. Ecclesiastes speaks of a season of all things. There is a season to be born, and a season to die. There is a season to mourn, and a season to rejoice.

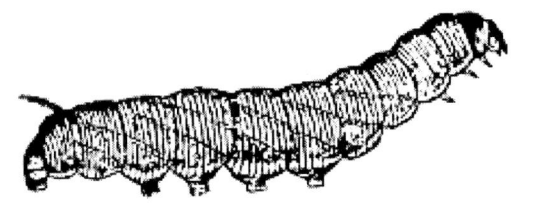

Ecclesiastes 3:1 *"To everything there is a season, and a time to every purpose under the heaven."*

So with it in the transformation process, you will see life to death and then brought back to life again. We are born in this world with the DNA of God inside of us and through our lives that DNA tends to be stretched and distorted. And this distortion brings about a confused, feared mind. This confused, feared mind begins to tell us we are something that we truly are not. So when the prophetic word of the Lord comes to us, it brings the transformation process, to give us life and life more abundantly. The life we were meant to have, now begins to manifest, and become our reality. God has got to get to the point of even changing our character and our very nature. We see that in the Scriptures when he deals with Abram becoming Abraham. We also see this transformation process take place within the life of Saul being transformed into a new life called Paul. When we take a look at Jacob, we see how Jacob had to wrestle not only with God, but also with himself.

Genesis 32:34 *"And Jacob was left alone; and there wrestled a man with him until the breaking of the day."*

In order to become Israel, Jacob had to be left alone and wrestle with a man. The wrestling process caused an awakening within Jacob to remove the leaders that he had placed upon himself and become the man that God had created him to be all along. Certain things within our lives must be broken down before they can be built up. When we look at the life of Jeremiah in the Bible, we notice how Jehovah God first rooted up things within Jeremiah's life. Then He began to plant or build up where he had previously rooted up. So you see, the process must start with an elimination before it can begin to build.

> **Prophetic Principle:**
>
> **Metamorphosis is A Transformation Factor.**

Meta-Morphosis

When we look at the prefix "meta," we notice it means "after, between or among." It literally means to "change in position."

God has to bring you to a repositioning, to get you to what He has declared over you in your life of what will be happening. He is setting you up for great victory. Even when we look at the letters "re" before a word, we have to remember that these two letters literally mean to "restore to its original state or form." We can look in the Bible at the words "restore," "renew" and "rebuild" and understand these words literally mean to "restore back to its original state and form."

So now we understand that through a prophetic word God desires for us to be restored, reconciled and rebuilt to our original state of how He created us to be on planet Earth. He desires for the life that has always been in us before our mother's womb to come alive again. And through a metamorphosis transformation process, the procedure will take us through the valley of not knowing who we really are and place our feet upon a firm foundation, which is the mountaintop of the Lord. There and only then will we each truly know our identity and why we were created. God has to alter our form and bring us to a place of redefining. Our spirits know who we really are, but because we are spirits having a human experience, the flesh tends to build walls between the people we think we are and the people we were meant to be.

We are and always have been spirits first. Religion has taught us long enough that we are trying to reach a place called the spirit but yet in reality you can never separate the authentic you, which is spirit from the place it's from. Metamorphosis begins as a seed which is the prophetic word of God. And even though you cannot see it with your natural eye and you cannot see the potential of the seed, you have to believe by faith that God is redefining you or getting you back to your original state of being.

> ### Prophetic Principle:
>
> Metamorphosis Means A Shift is Taking Place Inside.

It's very interesting to know that the present "me" I am, or think I am is actually the enemy to my prophetic word. The prophetic word, once spoken into my life, is there to awaken me to the Christ consciousness. The present "me" will wrestle with the authentic me I should be, simply because the flesh does not like change.

The flesh will always wrestle with change. We have to remember that before Apostle Paul was the apostle God awakened him to be, he was Saul; which means, Saul was the enemy of Paul. Because Saul killed and persecuted Christians and Paul loved, awakened and brought so many people to salvation through Christ. So we have to come to the conclusion that if you are not your authentic self, which means you have not been transformed by the renewing of your mind, walking in the fullness of your prophetic word then you may be the enemy to the authentic self, or the "you" God intended for you to be on planet Earth. Now for many of you, this might sound like a tongue twister but to those who have an ear to hear it will become life to you. We have to go beyond our natural scope and take an inner look to see the full result that the prophetic word is trying to get the external to move in. Remember, even the Lord himself told us that man looks on the outside, while God himself looks on the heart, or the inside. So God will always start with the inner before he deals with the outer. So the prophetic word will always deal with the inner, or the heart of man, before it deals with the outer. So once you receive the word of the Lord, you will not see a change on the outside at first. But if you have the eye of the Eagle, or what I like to call the eye of God, then you will see inwardly the movement and the transformation that has begun from within.

When we receive that seed, or the word of the Lord, we will not even see the seed being planted, because it will come forth in a specific time frame. But we have to believe by faith that God is up to something within us. When the seed or the word of the Lord is planted within us, many times a replication factor will take place from within.

1 Corinthians 3:9 *"For we are co-workers in God's service; you are God's field, God's building."*

The work has finally begun once we receive it by faith and walk on the water of the spirit. Sometimes the replication factor will leave us in a place of darkness where we can't even see our hand before our face. This means many people around us will not even be able to tell the nature of who we have been, or who we are actually becoming. This is because when we are being transformed in the middle of the metamorphosis process, we have no definition. Many times, you or others will not even be able to tell your own identity, or even your purpose anymore. Simply because you are in the middle or the meta of your process. We always have to remember it will take time for the process to finish. It is what I like to call the cocoon state of being. Everyone on planet Earth will go through a cocoon state of being. Even when we read in the Scriptures, we find out that in Christ there is neither male nor female. It even goes on to say there is neither bond nor free, Greek nor Jew.

Galatians 3:28 *"There is neither Jew nor Gentile, neither slave nor free, nor is there male and female, for you are all one in Christ Jesus."*

So, in Christ we take on a totally new definition, identity and purpose. This has and always will be our true identity. Are you ready to be awakened? Are you ready for the transformation process to begin? Are you ready to receive a word from the Lord that will change your life forever?

The Seed and the Egg Finally Collide

In the natural, when the seed of a man enters in the woman's womb, something begins to take place. When the seed and the egg come in contact with one another, a replication factor begins to take place. This is where the cells within her body begin to break down rapidly, and it begins to make its way towards its definition; which means, its image and purpose. Things will begin to break down rapidly within your life when you receive the seed of the Lord inside your spiritual womb.

You have to remember, any time you are in the presence of the Lord, you will receive an impartation. Receiving an impartation is powerful! Many times in your life the Lord will allow you to go through many different changes. It is the exact same thing when a surgeon or a doctor tries to determine the gender of the baby, but cannot. No matter how much they look at the tissue, they cannot figure out the gender of the baby unless there is some type of form or some type of definition. But they understand and know that through time they will find what they are looking for. They know that time must have its fervent course. The only person who knows who you really are and not what you've become is God Almighty. God holds the keys because He is the one that formed you, made you into his image and likeness, and knows your ending from the very beginning.

So in the middle of the metamorphosis process you will sometimes feel like you are just tissue with no definition. But within the tissue, lays the life, identity, gender and purpose of your life. So while you are in the waiting room of life, be still and know that He is God. God will take you from a seed conceived into a form revealed. When God speaks, there is a declaration of the end that begins simultaneously. It all begins and ends at the exact same time. And time can either be your friend or it will be your enemy. We have to let the seed develop naturally as God intended it to be. What I always share with people when I receive a prophetic word from the Lord is I now begin to be drawn or attracted to the magnet that the prophetic seed or word of the Lord is drawing me towards. You see, the prophetic word will always draw you like a magnet towards your destiny when you have an ear to hear and an eye to see. Allow your spirit, once receiving the word of the Lord, to draw you in the direction it needs to go in order to fulfill your life's purpose.

The Egg and its Incubation

When the egg is being fertilized by the mother hen, if you try to pick at the egg, you can possibly kill the chicken inside. But the chicken inside the egg must pick its own way out in the fullness of time. This means, when you are ready in your spirit to be the person God has created you to be, by previously receiving the instruction and direction that the prophetic word presented to you in your life, you will finally be the whole person God has created you to be. No one around you can pick at the shell and tell the chicken that it's time has come. Only the chicken inside the egg has a sense of awareness to know and understand the timing that life has begun. And when the fullness of time has come to you, you will know and understand that now is the time for me to finally live the life God has created for me to live.

Death Certificate and Birth Certificate all in One

When we receive the word of the Lord for our lives, we always must be ready to receive the death that the prophetic word will bring with it in order to receive the life that follows behind it.

We never stop to understand that in the Old Testament, the Lord told the people, *"I will strike and yet I will turn around and heal."*

Isaiah 19:22 *"The Lord will strike Egypt with a plague; he will strike them and heal them. They will turn to the Lord, and he will respond to their pleas and heal them."*

You see, God is in the ministry of exchange. The ministry of exchange means that something must be given in order to receive something else. So God will always come to you and ask you to give Him something in order for Him to give you what He desires for you to have.

Give Me All that You Have

When we take a look in the Old Testament, we find the prophet Elisha whom the Lord told to go to Zaraphath. There you will find a widow woman. Now at the time, Zaraphath was going through a great famine. So the widow woman was going to bake for herself and her son a cake. And once they ate the cake, they would die.

1 Kings 17:9-12 "Go at once to Zarephath in the region of Sidon and stay there. I have directed a widow there to supply you with food." 10 So he went to Zarephath. When he came to the town gate, a widow was there gathering sticks. He called to her and asked, "Would you bring me a little water in a jar so I may have a drink?" 11 As she was going to get it, he called, "And bring me, please, a piece of bread." 12 "As surely as the Lord your God lives," she replied, "I don't have any bread—only a handful of flour in a jar and a little olive oil in a jug. I am gathering a few sticks to take home and make a meal for myself and my son, that we may eat it—and die."

The widow woman understood that all she had in the natural was just a little bit left then nothing would remain ever again. So the widow woman was prepared to call it quits. Simply because her eyes were about the natural and not the spiritual. Because in the spirit there was already an abundance prepared for her but she did not have an ear to hear and an eye to see it. So God was going to send a prophet to take that last portion that the widow woman had in order to give her life and life more abundantly. You see, this is the way the kingdom of God works. God takes, in order for him to give back good measure, pressed down, shaken together and running over.

Luke 6:38 *"Give, and it will be given to you. A good measure, pressed down, shaken together and running over, will be poured into your lap. For with the measure you use, it will be measured to you."*

The kingdom of God will never give unless it first takes your very last breath away. Your very last morsel must be taken first before the feast is handed to you. It is called the ministry of exchange.

Isaiah 46:10 *"Declaring the end from the beginning, and from ancient times the things that are not yet done, saying, My counsel shall stand, and I will do all my pleasure."*

He understands before time began what needed to remain in our lives and what needed to be taken away. When Elisha approached the widow woman he told her to give him her last morsel by preparing and making him a cake. Could you imagine the expression upon that woman's face? But you see, the prophet that was carrying the word of the Lord in his belly knew it was time for the widow woman to enter into her metamorphosis process and be redefined.

When God's word is released into an atmosphere, there is a declaration of the death of one thing, and a new season of another beginning at the same time. God will come and hand you a death certificate, and when you receive that death certificate, then and only then will He give you the birth certificate. Often times it seems to even bring a state of confusion after the declaration. And sometimes that declaration might come in the form of instruction or direction. So don't ever assume the declaration of the prophetic word that God brings to your life will be what you want to hear or what you thought God would say to you.

Many times in my own life God has used me to speak into the life of thousands upon thousands of people, and I have seen many of those people look me in the eye and tell me these famous words, "I do not understand what was just spoken to me." You see, the declaration of the Lord that comes to us to change our lives is not meant for us to understand but it is meant for our spirits to leap with confirmation even when our flesh, or mind has no clue what was just spoken. It's not about what you know in the prophetic word that brings change to your life, it is about faith and knowing that you need a change from your present state or condition. It amazes me how many people will get frustrated when they hear the declaration or the prophetic word of the Lord that has just been spoken over their life because maybe it's not what they wanted to hear or they feel the word of the Lord is something they cannot obtain or reach high enough to fulfill. But yet, those same people will go home and cry and be miserable because they desire change. So when God approaches them to bring change, since it's not the change they were looking for, they tend to rebel and run the opposite direction. We have to remember that God's ways are higher than our ways and his thoughts are higher than our thoughts. This is simply a result of our minds not walking in the Christ conscious mind of God. When you walk in the mind of Christ, you will desire your change, no matter how it is presented to you.

> ### Prophetic Principle:
> We have to remember that through transformation comes death and life.

When a person is to the point of starvation, they do not care what you feed them. Even if it is spinach and they don't like spinach. A hungry person is not a picky person. In other words, when you hunger and thirst after righteousness, you will be filled. It is time that we get back to desiring what God wants for us and not what we want for ourselves.

Questions:
Part 6

1. Metamorphosis is a _____ _____.

2. Any time you receive something greater than the way you think, you will always be _____, plowed, and _____.

3. _____ means to change in form or nature.

4. Metamorphosis means a _____ is taking place inside.

5. Through a transformation or metamorphosis process, you will be changed into a ____ _____.

6. Everything in _____ has a cycle of life and death.

7. Genesis 32:34 "And Jacob was left alone; and there wrestled a bear and a lion until the breaking of the day." (T or F)

8. Sometimes the _____ _____ will leave us in a place of darkness where we can't even see our hand before our face.

9. When the egg is being _____ by the mother hen, if you try to pick at the egg, you can possibly _____ the chicken inside.

10. The _____ _____ _____ means that something must be given in order to receive something else.

CHRIST CONSCIOUSNESS

Christ Consciousness

So many people have asked me over the years, what does it mean when you say Christ consciousness? There are only two minds that reside on planet Earth.

You will either possess the mind of the world, which I call "limited," or you will possess the "unlimited" mind, called the mind of Christ, or the Christ conscious mind.

Romans 8:6 *"For to be carnally minded is death; but to be spiritually minded is life and peace."*

1 Corinthians 2:16 *"For who hath known the mind of the Lord, that he may instruct him? but we have the mind of Christ."*

When you operate by the means of the natural, you will always walk in a limited realm. Which means, you will fall short of the glory of God every time. When I say, you will fall short of the glory of God, I mean you will never reach the fullness of your potential or the reality of what God has in store for you to complete. Christ consciousness represents fullness, unlimited, never lacking, unspeakable joy, love, hope, grace, and anything that goes beyond the natural thinking of mankind. Christ consciousness is not something we walk in and out of. It is something where our minds are not only transformed but maintained to live 24 hours a day, seven days a week. Christ consciousness is not something you will obtain because you know a lot of Scriptures. It is not obtained because you speak in tongues. It is a way of life for those who understand that it is not by works lest any man should boast. It is a realm where you live, move and have your being.

> ### Prophetic Principle:
>
> We are spirits having a human experience and not humans having a supernatural spiritual experience.

My Destiny was Given to Me Before I was Born

Jeremiah's life was summed up from the very beginning. From the very beginning even within the book of Jeremiah, his purpose was spoken about concerning his life. The beginning of Jeremiah tells us something amazing about Jeremiah:

Jeremiah 1:4-5 *"Then the word of the Lord came unto me, saying, 'Before I formed thee in the belly*

I knew thee; and before thou camest forth out of the womb I sanctified thee, and I ordained thee a prophet unto the nations.'"

The word "knew" in the original Aramaic, literally means, "impartation, intimacy and intercourse." It's the same word we see in the book of Genesis where Adam "knew" Eve.

Genesis 4:1 *"And Adam knew Eve his wife; and she conceived, and bare Cain, and said, "I have gotten a man from the Lord.'"*

It means before each and every one of us on planet Earth came into our mother's womb, we had the DNA of God already inside of us. We came preprogrammed in this life before we ever came out of our mother's womb. Every one of us in this life, go through this life and never have a clue what we are called to do. So God raises up the means by using the dimensions of the prophetic to speak that which was, and that which is, and that which is to come and wraps it all up within a prophetic word. In dealing with the prophetic word, we deal with an awakening spirit. When a prophetic word is received within the heart of man, it begins to awaken something that has always been there and always will be there, even though it is asleep. The prophetic word comes to awaken the life from within and reminds that person there is hope and a bright future within you.

John 1:9 *"That was the true Light, which lighteth every man that cometh into the world."*

This means, there is a light within humanity, yet humanity does not see it, nor understand that there is a light in the midst of their darkness. So you see, there is a light within people yet people cannot see it because their eyes have not been anointed with eye salve, so they can see so they end up *"suffering from a lack of knowledge"* as the bible states.

Hosea 4:6 *"My people are destroyed for lack of knowledge...."*

In the book of Revelation, the Lord spoke to a specific church, and reminded that the church cannot see into the spirit realm because their eyes have not been anointed yet.

Revelation 3:18 *"I counsel thee to buy of me gold tried in the fire, that thou mayest be rich; and white raiment, that thou mayest be clothed, and that the shame of thy nakedness do not appear; and anoint thine eyes with eye salve, that thou mayest see."*

This means, we all need ears to hear, and eyes to see. So just because you have a natural eye, and a natural year, does not mean you know what lies within you already. Some things come strictly through prayer and fasting. And some things come through a revelation, or an enlightenment. I have heard it said, or called an "ah-ha moment." No matter what we call it, we all must be awakened by something higher than ourselves; which is the Lord.

So you see, a prophetic word comes to awaken the heart, and causes it to truly start beating with the rhythm of heaven. It comes to remind us, there is a seed or a light within you. I have heard it said by many, "it bears witness with me," or they will say "that confirms with my spirit." This means, many people, when receiving a prophetic word for their lives, it bears witness within them. What exactly does that mean?

> ### Prophetic Principle:
>
> The Mind of Christ is A Mind of Motion and Movement. When You have His Mind, you will be in the Flow of that Movement.

It means they might not understand the prophetic word in its fullness, but something in them reminds them this word is true and right for you. When a prophetic word comes into a person's life, and it bears witness with them, it means the DNA of God that has always been in them, even before the world began, cries out and says, "this awakens me."

The Mind and the Prophetic

I wanted to incorporate within the **School of the Prophets** course, the power of the mind and how it relates to the prophetic. I believe the mind is very powerful. The mind determines every walk, every step in everything we do in our lives. The mind is so powerful that when we think a thought concerning moving our legs, our arms or even getting mad, our body has to respond to the command of our thought. The mind thinks it and the body does it. It is said that we are controlled by the thoughts we think. In other words, my mind must think a thought first and then my body through action, carries out the thought. Until that thought eventually becomes the reality. So in order to understand the gift or office of the prophetic, we must understand how the mind works. God speaks to our spirit first the word of the Lord. Then He uses our mind to show us picture forms and words within a split second in order for us to translate to the person what is being conveyed in the message.

> ### Prophetic Principle:
>
> The First Mind is called the Christ Conscious Mind. The Second Mind is called the Sin Conscious Mind. You will Walk in One or the Other.

I mentioned in the first course of the **School of the Prophets**, the difference between the seer and the prophet. Even though a seer is a prophet, not all prophets are seers. Now in dealing with the Ministry of the seer, we see that the main strength for the seer is that they will see images and picture forms within their imagination and their mind. So truly thoughts do become things. We must be careful when we operate within the prophetic ministry to keep our minds guarded and fixed upon things that are holy, pure, creative and things that are of a good report. The mind is so powerful that when it gets an image within the subconscious mind, it waits for us to respond to give action so it can grow and ultimately become not only a mindset, but an idol. Idols or mindsets are things that begin to take root within the subconscious mind that do not belong. From that moment on, you will not make a move unless you consult the mindset or idol first.

In the Old Testament, the Bible speaks very clear about not having any idols in place of the Lord or what I like to call, anything that is in the path of the Lord's will for your life. Tear down the idol (walls) that are holding you back from seeing your promise land.

> *Prophetic Principle:*
>
> When I was Born, My Mind was Programmed for Success.

While many today look upon the outside to find a natural substance or thing that would be considered an idol but yet God makes it very plain that he looks not on the outside, but looks at the heart. God knows what goes into a man must come out of a man. When the mind feeds on a thought and we begin to give it our attention, it begins to multiply, produce and grow. God has created you to be fruitful and multiply.

Genesis 1:22 *"And God blessed them, saying, Be fruitful, and multiply, and fill the waters in the seas, and let fowl multiply in the earth."*

So whatever you desire in your life, think about it and you shall have it.

"As a man thinketh in his heart so is he."

To put it another way: everything in life starts with a thought (idea) first.

Everything around us in creation begins by someone having a thought. A thought is something you cannot see with the natural eye. You cannot hear with the natural ear. But yet it is more real than anything we can ever behold with our eyes and ears in the natural. If everything in creation starts with a thought first, that means we must be careful what we think about. So in dealing with the prophetic voice of the Lord, we must understand God speaks to our mind first and as the vessels of the Lord, we use our mouth to begin to prophesy the word of the Lord. Now when I say the term, prophetic imagination, I mean every person on planet Earth is prophetic in nature simply because there is the power of a thought planted within mankind, which is the power of creativity; which means men and women every single day of their lives create through the power of imagination, and all it takes or begins with is a small seed that we call a thought. Thoughts are nothing more than a seed planted within the mind. God gave us a mind because he wanted us to be like him by having the mind of Christ which means, your mind is preprogrammed to create, multiply and produce.

> ### Prophetic Principle:
>
> Since God knows the Ending from our Beginning, He Knows what Needs to Stay and what Needs to Go.

The Law of Movement

The law of movement is a universal law. It is a law that God set into motion before time began. The law of movement means everything that God creates or is creating by the spoken word out of his mouth, meaning everything in creation must be in a constant evolving or moving or flow. Everything in creation is always in movement.

Acts 17:28 *"For in him we live, and move, and have our being...."*

Everything evolves, grows and shifts. If you're in Christ, you will "move." So you see, if everything in creation grows and evolves; it does that simply because it comes from a mind that is in constant movement. Your mind never stays still, it is always in a constant flow of giving and taking.

Scientists say that everyone thinks between 60 to 65 thousand thoughts a day.

So the mind is in constant movement to receive thoughts that come and go but yet the authentic true nature of who you are has the power to either give life to the seed (of thought) or reject it and cause it to move on.

The Power of Light and Energy

Every time we begin to focus and pay our attention on a thought in our brain, we stir up energy and send it out to the atmosphere. Now you might say, that sounds a little too New Age for me. But I want to assure you that it is a known fact that everything in creation is energy or light slowed down into matter. It is a scientific proof and also a fact within the word of God.

Jesus said, *"you are the light of the world."*

This means, He knew our original state of being is that of light. And yet every time we draw closer to truth or revelation of who we are in Christ, we begin to accelerate the process of getting back to the original state in which we were created to be.

> ### Prophetic Principle:
>
> The Power of Attention thrusts your Prophetic Thoughts to Become a Quicker Reality.

"Let there be Light."

Genesis 1:3 *"And God said, Let there be light: and there was light."*

Every time you begin to have an awakening through the word of the Lord, you begin to draw the spirit realm closer to you.

Psalms 17:15 *"When I awake, I will be satisfied with seeing your likeness."*

You begin to make your creative thoughts manifest in the natural world. You see, focused attention on a thought by not wavering or straying from your focus, and continuing to stand in faith, empowers the thought to grow. It is time for us to begin to stir up our creative energy and ability to call those things that be not as though they are.

Romans 4:17 *"God, who quickeneth the dead, and calleth those things which be not as though they were."*

I believe in the law of manifestation, by fully focusing your entire attention, energy and prayer upon the very substance or thought that comes from the heavenlies that is sitting within your brain desiring to move, but is waiting on you to give it a command in the direction it needs to go. Every time we begin to focus our full attention upon the word of the Lord, or the visual (dream) that God has placed within our minds, we begin to see the flame become an all-consuming fire. This means, the power of attention thrusts your prophetic thoughts to become reality quicker. Remember, the word of the Lord lets us know that what we think about, we become.

The Law of Becoming

The law of becoming involves the thought process within mankind. When we look at the book of Genesis, we notice it is the first book of the Bible simply because Genesis means the beginning. And everything in creation has a beginning. Everything has a beginning and an end.

Everything lives and dies. The law of becoming starts with the thought process. So we have a thought, believe in our heart that it shall come to pass, and give our full attention to that prophetic thought and the law of manifestation and the law of becoming begins to be activated.

Mark 11:23 *"For verily I say unto you, That whosoever shall say unto this mountain, Be thou removed, and be thou cast into the sea; and shall not doubt in his heart, but shall believe that those things which he saith shall come to pass; he shall have whatsoever he saith."*

Whether we see it or feel it or know it, the law of becoming and the law of manifestation are in constant work and motion within our lives. Since these two laws are in constant motion within creation, we must realize the importance of the power of the mind and thoughts. This is why the Lord tells us to consume ourselves with the mind of Christ. When we begin to work in the mind of Christ, we will know that our thoughts will flow from a pure stream and push us closer to the will of God. So my thoughts begin to become his thoughts. And his thoughts begin to manifest within my life because I have allowed the law of exchange to take place at that moment.

This means, I begin to exchange my mind for the mind of Christ. And the true identity of myself in which the natural tends to move into is only a result of what the mind of Christ has willed for me before time began. Therefore, when the law of manifestation begins to kick in, I not only become what He has originally created for me to be, I finally begin to behold what my mind for so long has kept locked up as a thought within the back of my spirit. So the thought within my subconscious begins to be hovered over by my attention just like Mary was hovered over by the Holy Spirit.

So my attention hovers over the thought and begins to empower it and causes it to grow, produce and manifest through the law of becoming.

> ### Prophetic Principle:
>
> Everything Originates from A Thought.

It is so important for us to possess the mind of Christ whether we move in the prophetic or not. But when we do move in the prophetic gift, we must understand how the mind and thoughts operate and also understand the process of the law of becoming. Once we see it or think it we are held accountable for what we see, hear and think. And once we gain understanding of the process of the mind, it will begin to work for us and not against us. God uses every spiritual gift in His word according to the pattern and laws that He has set into motion to govern the universe. We have to remember that He said in His word that He honors His word above His own name.

Psalms 138:2 "*I will worship toward thy holy temple, and praise thy name for thy lovingkindness and for thy truth: for thou hast magnified thy word above all thy name.*"

Isaiah 40:22 "*He sits enthroned above the circle of the earth, and its people are like grasshoppers. He stretches out the heavens like a canopy, and spreads them out like a tent to live in.*"

Remember, you will behold and become what you give your full attention to. The power of attention governs our entire life. At this very moment, you are involved in **The School of the Prophets Advanced Course** simply because you had a thought and empowered the thought by giving it your attention and your desire. Attention and desire go hand and hand.

The word says that creation moans and groans because it awaits for the sons of God to manifest.

Romans 8:19 *"For the earnest expectation of creation waiteth for the manifestation of the sons of God."*

Romans 8:22 *"For we know that the whole creation groaneth and travaileth in pain together until now."*

I share with many people on a daily basis that I encounter in my life coaching sessions, that the Lord uses creation (universe) to "help us" get where we need to be in the will of God (our destiny) by drawing things to us to "take notice" in and give it ATTENTION. You see, if the universe or creation pushes us closer to our destiny, which is the perfect will of God for our lives, it begins to be released from the curse that was placed upon it by Adam.

Give attention to the things the Lord brings in the details of your life. It is with the small things that the Lord watches you to see how you will treat it. You will not understand or be promoted to the big things until you are faithful with the small things (thoughts). Feed and empower your prophetic thoughts with the power of attention so they will grow up and mature into the image the Lord desires them to be according to His plan and purpose for your life.

Philippians 2:13 *"For it is God which worketh in you both to will and to do of his good pleasure."*

Prophetic Principles:

Good Ideas are Limited. God Ideas are Unlimited.

Questions:
Part 7

1. Everything originates from a _____.

2. The mind of man is _____. The mind of God is _____.

3. The word _____ in the original Aramaic, literally means, "impartation, intimacy and intercourse."

4. The _____ ____ _____ thrusts your prophetic thoughts to become a quicker reality.

5. Psalms 17:15 *"When I read the word, I will be satisfied with seeing your likeness."* (T or F)

6. Every time we begin to _____ our _____ _____ upon the word of the Lord, or the visual (dream) that God has placed within our minds, we begin to see the flame become an all-consuming fire.

7. When we begin to work in the mind of Christ, we will know that our thoughts will flow from a _____ _____ and push us closer to the will of God.

8. Attention and _____ go hand and hand.

9. God uses every _____ _____ in his word according to the pattern and laws that He has set into motion to govern the universe. (He has set the universe like a canopy by His hand.)

10. God uses _____ to draw us closer to our destiny in Him.

THE PROCESS OF PROPHETIC LEADING

The Life of Abraham

When we take a look at the life of Abraham, we see a man who was formally called Abram and is now called Abraham. We see a man previously that did not know the purpose of God nor the plans of God for his life. When God spoke to Abram and called him to be Abraham, the father of many nations; He gave Abraham purpose again. When Abraham received the word of the Lord, his life took him on a course in which he had no clue where he would end up. You see, before Abraham's name changed, all he ever produced was Ishmael. It wasn't the fact that Ishmael was a bad person, it just means that God's ultimate first original plan for Abraham, was to produce an Isaac.

So before our metamorphosis transformation process, we will always find ourselves producing Ishmaels. And Ishmael is what I consider to be limited; coming from the natural realm humanity. But yet Isaac was from a seed that was not necessarily from this world. Even though it was the seed of an older gentleman named Abraham, its purpose was not from the natural lineage of Abraham. It's call had a higher purpose and plan. The Bible says, that the latter shall be greater than the former.

Haggai 2:9 *"The glory of this present house will be greater than the glory of the former house, says the Lord Almighty."*

This means, what we could produce before the word of the Lord in our lives was a good idea, but not a god idea.

They take you as high and as far as you ever thought or dreamed possible you could go. Well your life goes through many changes and courses during the metamorphosis transformation process, you need to learn to be honest with yourself and admit you have no clue what might be going on inside of you.

Psalm 46:10 *"Be still, and know that I am God; I will be exalted among the nations, I will be exalted in the earth."*

But continue to hold on, reach out and look up knowing your redemption draws nigh to you.

Prophetic Principle:

When you Walk in Prophetic Awareness, You will Speak the Words, *"Let there Be Light"* to Creation.

Luke 21:28 *"When these things begin to take place, stand up and lift up your heads, because your redemption is drawing near."*

Abraham found in his life that he could not go any further, until he gave in to the life of God.

The Life of David

David's life was full of adventure. He went from tending sheep in the field to being a king in Israel. His life was full of betrayal, deceit and murder. Yet in every area of David's life, he knew how to reach out to the prophets and the hand of God. As David was tending his father's sheep in the field, he had no clue or no dream of ever being a king in a kingdom. But yet his metamorphosis process, later on in his life took him, and taught him to be the greatest king that ever lived.

I Samuel 17:37 *"The Lord who rescued me from the paw of the lion and the paw of the bear will rescue me from the hand of this Philistine."*

David went from fighting a lion and a bear in the field, to being in prophetic rulership.

Called to be a Prophet or Seer?

In First Samuel chapter 9 verse nine, we read,

"Let us go to the seer, for he that is now called a prophet, was before time a seer."

This means, many times when you receive the prophetic word of the Lord, you perceive things, but don't have the ability to speak them. You know you can see, but you don't have the ability to become. Many times in my own life, when the prophetic word of the Lord was planted within my spirit, I found myself seeing that but not being able to speak it. I watched throughout the years, how so many people know something is going on inside of their spirit from the Lord, but can't seem to put it into words. It is as if you have seen a great phenomenon, or felt something you have never felt before, and you try to describe it to people, but you do not have the natural words to formulate to make them understand what's going on inside of you.

Let Go of the Normal

In Romans chapter 12 verse two, it reads:

"Be not conformed to this world, but be ye transformed by the renewing of your mind."

The prophetic word of the Lord will come to you to transform your life out of the normal, humanistic mind of man, and teach you how to embrace the "new" that you have never known before.

Isaiah 43:19 *"Behold, I will do a new thing; now it shall spring forth; shall ye not know it? I will even make a way in the wilderness, and rivers in the desert."*

The "new things" come from the mouth of God. If you want to change your life and leave the mundane way you have been living, you will only find it in the mouth of God.

Remember this: that fear will always short-circuit the process that the prophetic word has begun inside of you. Fear is a killer.

2 Timothy 1:7 *"For God hath not given us the spirit of fear; but of power, and of love, and of a sound mind."*

It stops the flow of the life of God through the prophetic word within your life. Transformation comes from a time of isolation in your incubation. It is required of you to be isolated away from the "feared you" you have become by others so you can become the "authentic you" that you were created to be. Leave the "feared you" behind so the "authentic you" can shine forth in the realm of "new things."

Mark 2:22 *"And no man putteth new wine into old bottles: else the new wine doth burst the bottles, and the wine is spilled, and the bottles will be marred: but new wine must be put into new bottles."*

The transformation process is something we all go through if submitted to the Lord's will for our lives. It is required if we intend to continue to press towards the mark of the high prize in Christ Jesus.

Philippians 3:14 *"I press toward the mark for the prize of the high calling of God in Christ Jesus."*

Ruth and Boaz

In the story of Ruth and Boaz, we see where Ruth, before marrying Boaz, had to go to the threshing floor. The threshing floor was a place of purifying, sanctifying and cleansing. I like to call it the place where God separated the "wheat from the tares" inside of Ruth.

Ruth 3:1 *"One day Ruth's mother-in-law Naomi said to her, 'My daughter, I must find a home for you, where you will be well provided for. 2 Now Boaz, with whose women you have worked, is a relative of ours. Tonight he will be winnowing barley on the threshing floor. 3 Wash, put on perfume, and get dressed in your best clothes. Then go down to the threshing floor, but don't let him know you are there until he has finished eating and drinking. 4 When he lies down, note the place where he is lying. Then go and uncover his feet and lie down. He will tell you what to do.'*
5 'I will do whatever you say,' Ruth answered. 6 So she went down to the threshing floor and did everything her mother-in-law told her to do.
7 When Boaz had finished eating and drinking and was in good spirits, he went over to lie down at the far end of the grain pile. Ruth approached quietly, uncovered his feet and lay down. 8 In the middle of the night something startled the man; he turned - and there was a woman lying at his feet!"

When we look at all of these and many other stories in the bible, we remember that in order to be used by God, we will be transformed, stripped and go through the much needed stages the Lord will require for us to go through in order to deliver His powerful word to others.

If you want to be a leader, you must be a great servant. Prophets and prophetic voices must awaken to purpose, walk in awareness and be stripped of "self" in order to resurrect into the Christ Nature.

Questions:
Part 8

1. When God spoke to Abram and called him to be a farmer in the field; He gave Abraham purpose again. (T or F)

2. Before our metamorphosis transformation process, we will always find ourselves producing _____.

3. David went from fighting a _____ and a _____ in the field, to being in prophetic rulership.

4. Many times when you receive the prophetic word of the Lord, you perceive things, but don't have the ability to _____ them.

5. The "new things" come from the _____ __ _____. If you want to change your life and leave the mundane way you have been living, you will only find it in the _____ ____ _____.

6. _____ will always short-circuit the process that the prophetic word has begun inside of you.

7. Leave the _____ _____ behind so the "authentic you" can shine forth in the realm of "new things."

8. Before Ruth married Boaz, she had to go to the _____ _____.

9. If you want to be a leader, you must be a great _____.

10. Describe in your own words how you want to see the word of the Lord change in your life.
_____
_____

Notes

Notes

Notes

Other books by Jeremy Lopez:

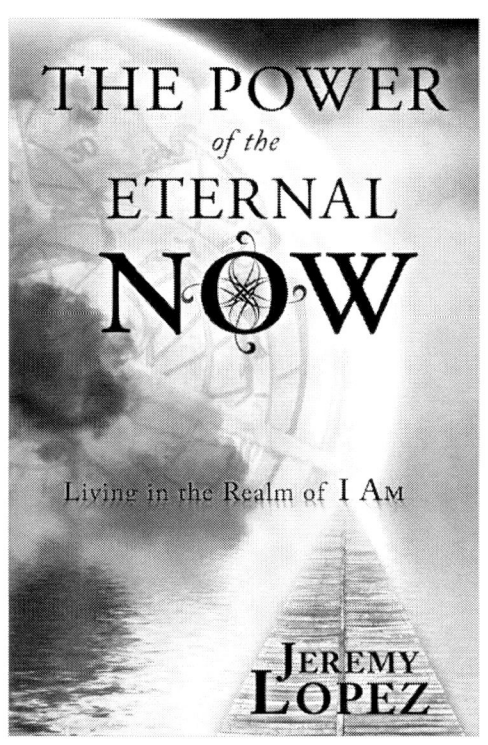

The Power of the Eternal Now

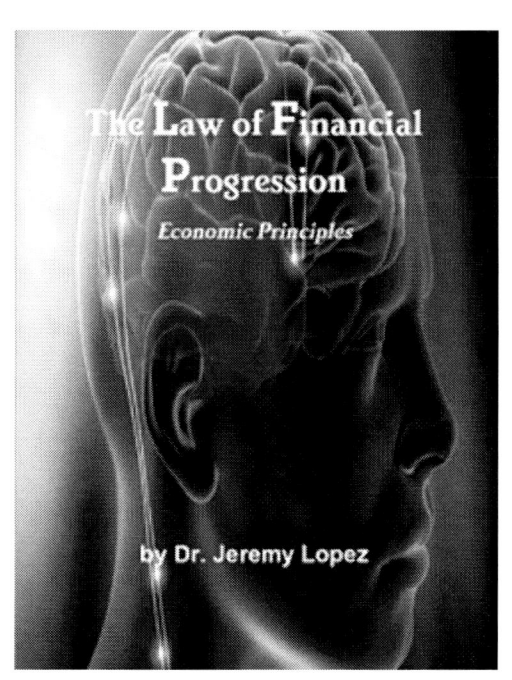

The Laws of Financial Progression

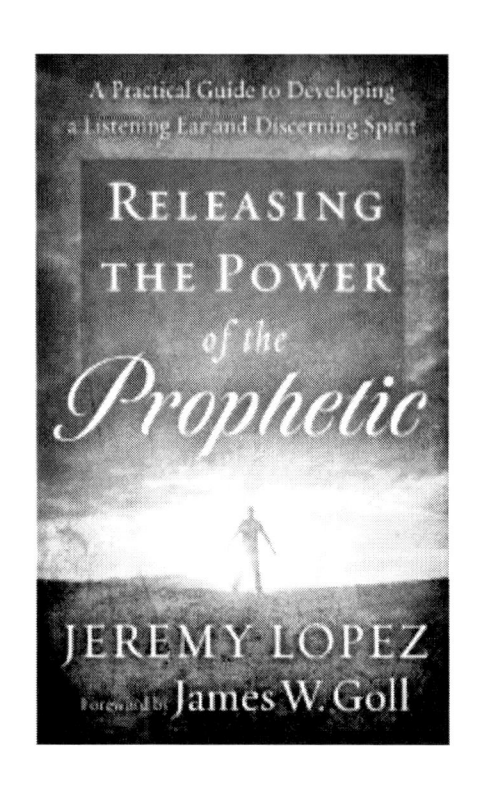

**Releasing the Power of the Prophetic:
A Practical Guide to Developing a Listening Ear and Discerning Spirit**

Jeremy Lopez also has over 50 teaching CDs.

For more information on all the teaching CDs and books by Jeremy Lopez, please visit: www.identitynetwork.net.

School of the Prophets Advanced Course

Diving Into the Mysteries of the Prophetic

BY DR. JEREMY LOPEZ

THE TRAINING MANUAL FOR THE SCHOOL OF THE PROPHETS